Italian Americans

SPIRIT
of America®

Italian AMERICANS

By Vicky Franchino

The Child's World®
Chanhassen, Minnesota

Italian AMERICANS

Published in the United States of America by The Child's World®
PO Box 326 • Chanhassen, MN 55317-0326 • 800-599-READ • www.childsworld.com

Acknowledgments

The Child's World®: Mary Berendes, Publishing Director

Editorial Directions, Inc.: E. Russell Primm, Emily Dolbear, Sarah E. De Capua, and Lucia Raatma, Editors; Linda S. Koutris, Photo Selector; Image Select International, Photo Research; Red Line Editorial and Pam Rosenberg, Fact Research; Tim Griffin/IndexServ, Indexer; Donna Frassetto, Proofreader

Photos

Cover/frontispiece: An Italian immigrant family on a ferry from the docks to Ellis Island, 1905

Cover photographs ©: Getty Images; ImageState, Inc.

Interior photographs ©: Corbis, 6, 7; Ann Ronan Picture Library, 8 top, 8 bottom; Culver Pictures, 9; AKG-Images, Berlin, 10, 11 top; Getty Images, 11 bottom, 12 top; AKG-Images, Berlin, 12 bottom; Corbis, 14; Getty Images, 15, 16; AKG-Images, Berlin, 16 bottom; Corbis, 17; Getty Images, 19; AKG-Images, Berlin, 20; Corbis, 22 top, 22 bottom; Getty Images, 23; Ann Ronan Picture Library, 24 top; Cinema Bookshop, 24 centre, 25 bottom; Corbis, 25 top, 25 bottom; AKG-Images, Berlin, 26 top; Getty Images, 26 bottom; Corbis, 27; Getty Images, 28.

Registration

The Child's World®, Spirit of America®, and their associated logos are the sole property and registered trademarks of The Child's World®.

Library of Congress Cataloging-in-Publication Data
Franchino, Vicky.
  Italian Americans / by Vicky Franchino.
     p. cm.
  Includes index.
  Summary: Provides a simple overview of the heritage, customs, and beliefs of Italian Americans and presents the accomplishments of some well-known Italian Americans.
   ISBN 1-56766-153-X (lib. bd. : alk. paper)
   1. Italian Americans—Juvenile literature. [1. Italian Americans.] I. Title.
   E184.I8 F73 2002
   973'.0451—dc21
                        2001007806

11   15   22

Contents

Chapter ONE

A Hard Life in Italy

ITALIANS HAVE BEEN COMING TO AMERICA FOR more than 500 years. Most immigrated between 1880 and 1930. Today, more than 15 million Americans have **ancestors** who came from Italy.

The first Italians came to America when it was still a **colony** of England. Many came from northern and central Italian cities such as Florence, Rome, Naples, and Venice. These early **immigrants** brought useful skills to America. They were weavers, gardeners, cabinetmakers, musicians, artisans, and businesspeople.

Workers at Buena Vista Vineyard, Sonoma, California, in the 1870s

During the early 1800s, more northern Italians moved to the United States. Many were successful farmers. They moved to the West Coast. The weather there was similar to Italy's. In California, they opened orchards, vegetable farms, and wineries.

In the 1880s, a different kind of Italian immigrant started to come to the United States. These people were poor Italians from the southern part of the country—an area known as the *Mezzagiorno,* which means "midday sun." These immigrants had little or no education. Many could not read. Nearly all of them were farmers.

The people of the Mezzagiorno had always had a difficult life. In the late 1800s, it became harder.

These Italians came to America because they believed there was no hope of a better life for them and their families in Italy. Many worked on land that was owned by wealthy families. Even farmers who owned their own

Some Italians lived in poverty in their native country.

7

land did not have an easy life. The soil in Southern Italy was poor, and most crops didn't grow well.

Life was hard for these poor farmers. Many families lived in simple one-room houses. They often shared their homes with their livestock. They had no indoor plumbing and some had to cook outside.

For centuries, Italy had been a divided land. In 1870, it became one country for the first time. The people of the Mezzagiorno hoped the new leader—Giuseppe Garibaldi—would make their life better. Instead, he raised their taxes and ignored their problems.

The people of southern Italy had other troubles, too. **Drought** ruined many of their crops. Plant lice destroyed their vineyards. In addition, sickness caused horrible

Italian leader Guiseppe Garibaldi

Government ministers visiting a hospital during the cholera epidemic in Naples

8

suffering. A **cholera** epidemic killed more than 55,000 people. Malaria, a disease carried by mosquitoes, killed many others.

The poor were worn out by these hardships. They dreamed of a better life. Many believed there was only one way for their dreams to come true. They must go to America.

This was not an easy decision. In those days, most people were born, married, and died in the same village. They didn't know what life would be like in America. Those who left Italy knew they might never return.

Leaving Italy was not an easy decision, but one that many citizens chose to make.

Chapter TWO

A New Life in America

Immigrants crowded into the steerage section of a ship headed to America.

ITALIANS CAME TO AMERICA ACROSS THE Atlantic Ocean by boat. The trip was long and difficult. It took two to four weeks. Most of the Italian immigrants traveled in steerage—it was all they could afford. This meant they slept in the bottom of the boat. It was crowded, dark, and dirty there.

Often there were not enough beds for all the immigrants. The passengers took turns sleeping. Sometimes the travelers had to supply their own food, too. There were not enough bathrooms and there was almost no privacy. In steerage, sickness spread quickly.

The travelers did not know what to expect when they reached America. They did not speak English. Very few had a family or a job waiting for them. Most immigrants were short of money. All they had was hope.

Many Italians landed in New York. In 1892, Ellis Island opened. This was a small island in New York Harbor. Immigrants were examined there before they were allowed into the United States.

The journey across the Atlantic was long, but many Italian families endured it.

As many as 5,000 people went through inspection at Ellis Island every day. The first step was a checkup. Doctors looked for signs of illness. Sometimes the doctor marked a person's shoulder with a chalk mark. This meant the immigrant needed to be examined more carefully.

Italian men newly arrived at Ellis Island in 1905

Next, the immigrants were asked questions: How old are you? What kind of job can you do? Do you have any money? Although most Italians passed this inspection, some were sent back to Italy.

Italian Americans celebrating a Catholic feast day in New York City's Little Italy

Many Italian Americans helped build U.S. railroads.

Many immigrants stayed in New York City. Most did not have enough money to travel farther. And they knew the city was a good place to find a job.

Italians tended to settle down together. The areas where they lived were called "Little Italy." The new immigrants could hear their own language there. They could find the food they were used to. They could celebrate their religious holidays.

Sometimes it was hard for Italian immigrants to find work. Many knew only how to farm. In the United States, they often did the hardest and most dangerous jobs. They built bridges, roads, and houses. They worked in mines and cut stone in quarries.

The new immigrants did their best to create a good life for themselves. They worked hard. They saved their money. Their families were at the center of everything they did.

The Italian Americans never forgot the life they had left behind. They tried to combine the best of their old life in Italy with the best of their new life in America.

THE TERRIBLE HARDSHIPS OF THE 1880S CAUSED MANY ITALIANS to dream of moving to America. The steam engine helped make their dreams come true. Before the steam engine, the trip across the Atlantic Ocean was slow, dangerous, and expensive. Ships were slower and smaller. They needed good weather for travel. With the steam engine, however, ships could carry larger loads. They did not need wind to move them across the ocean. It was still a long and difficult journey, but it was much shorter than it had been before.

Decade	Number of Italian Immigrants to the United States
1821–1830	439
1831–1840	2,253
1841–1850	1,870
1851–1860	9,231
1861–1870	11,725
1871–1880	55,759
1881–1890	307,309
1891–1900	651,893
1901–1910	2,045,877
1911–1920	1,109524
1921–1930	455,315
1931–1940	68,028
1941–1950	57,661

Chapter THREE

Facing New Challenges

An Italian-American family celebrating a birthday in New York

As ITALIAN AMERICANS adapted to life in America, they faced many changes. Some of the biggest changes took place in their own families.

In Italy, the father was the head of the house. He made all the important decisions for the family. He earned money and supported everyone. In Italy, the mother stayed at home. She took care of the house and the family. She had no other job. In Italy, children honored their parents. They followed the old customs. In America, things were different.

In America, the father did not always feel as if he was in charge. An Italian father might

14

not know how to speak English. He sometimes had to ask his children for help. In America, mothers often worked in factories to help support their families. In America, Italian-American children were sometimes embarrassed by their parents. They seemed old-fashioned and different. The children wanted to be American, not Italian.

Italian immigrants faced **prejudice** and **discrimination**. Many people worried about these new immigrants. They were afraid the newcomers would take their jobs. They thought the immigrants would change the country with their strange ways. They forgot their own families had once been immigrants, too!

Most Americans did not know much about Italians. Some people believed all Italians belonged to the Mafia. The Mafia is a secret group of criminals. While a few Italians were members of the Mafia, most were not.

Some people were uncomfortable with the

Italian-American gangster Al Capone (center), whose reputation hurt the image of Italians in the United States

Many Protestant Americans did not understand the practices of the Roman Catholic religion.

Italian leader Benito Mussolini

Italians' religion. The Roman Catholic religion was different from the more common Protestant religions practiced in America.

As the years passed, Italian immigrants began to feel they were truly Americans. They did well in their jobs. Many moved away from the East Coast where they had first settled.

World War II (1939–1945) was a time of change for Italian Americans. In 1922, Benito Mussolini became the leader of Italy. Some Italian Americans believed Mussolini would help the poor people of Italy. As they learned more about him, though, they realized that his government would hurt the poor.

When Mussolini brought Italy into World War II in 1940, Italy was on Germany's side. So, Italy was then an enemy of the United States. Most Italian Americans were shocked. They sided with their new country. More than 500,000 Italian Americans fought for the United States after America entered the war in 1941. Many of them fought in Italy. They saw the land of their fathers for the first time. They saw that many Italians still had a hard life. They understood why their parents had gone to America.

After the war, many Italian Americans were able to go to college because of the **GI Bill**. This government program gave former soldiers enough money to go to school. A college education helped many Italian Americans to get better jobs.

Today, Italian Americans live throughout the United States. Italians have changed in their "new country," but they have kept many important things from the "old country." Their families, their religion, and their traditions are still important parts of their life.

Today's Italian Americans still take pride in their background.

The Catholic Church in Italy sent Italian priests and nuns to America to help poor Italian immigrants. One of them was a nun named Mother Frances Xavier Cabrini. She arrived in New York City in 1889. She saw that people needed

help. They needed jobs and medical care. Mother Cabrini taught women how to embroider. They could use this skill to earn money. She set up a nursery so that poor children would have a safe place to go. Mother Cabrini saved money for a hospital. She asked doctors to work there without being paid. She called the hospital Columbus Hospital. Today, seven Columbus Hospitals are still open. They

still help the poor. Mother Cabrini died in 1917 (her body is shown here lying in state at Mother Cabrini High School in New York City). In 1946, the Catholic Church declared her a saint. She was the first U.S. citizen to become a saint.

Chapter FOUR

Changing America

AMERICA IS A LAND OF IMMIGRANTS. EACH group has brought its own foods, its own traditions, and its own way of life. Over time, many of these "old country" ways have become the American way.

Vineyards in California's Napa Valley

Italians have been part of America from its earliest days as a country. In the 1600s, colonists invited Italian winegrowers and glassmakers to move to America. The early Americans valued these skills and wanted to learn them from the people who did them best. Other Italians came and opened schools that taught writing, painting, and dancing.

A view inside the Capitol Rotunda, which was painted by Italian-American Constantino Brumidi in 1865

Italians also influenced the young country in more important ways. Thomas Jefferson wrote the Declaration of Independence. He turned to an Italian physician and merchant named Philip Mazzei for help in making America an independent country.

Mazzei wrote, "All men are by nature equally free and independent. Such equality is necessary in order to create a free government." His **philosophy** inspired Jefferson. In the Declaration of Independence, Jefferson wrote, "We hold these truths to be self-evident, that all men are created equal. . . ."

Many of the buildings in Washington, D.C., were influenced by Italian design. The U.S. Capitol was decorated by an Italian— Constantino Brumidi. Brumidi spent 20 years creating the inside of the Capitol. His beautiful paintings, staircases, and statues are still there today.

Well-known Italian foods include pasta, olives, sun-dried tomatoes, and Parmesan cheese.

Baseball legend Joe DiMaggio

Italians also shared their love of music. Early immigrants brought the violin, the viola, and the mandolin. Lorenzo da Ponte came to the United States in 1805. He was one of the people who helped start the Italian Opera House in New York City.

Italian farmers brought new foods to the United States. Artichokes, zucchini, and broccoli all came from Italy. Early winemakers used their skills to make California one of the leading wine-making states.

Some of the most popular foods in America first came from Italy. Pizza and salami are Italian. So are mozzarella, ravioli, and cappuccino. Today, these foods are almost more American than Italian!

Italians contributed to American culture in many other ways. Joe DiMaggio was one of the most famous baseball players in history. He played for the New York Yankees. DiMaggio set a record for hitting in 56 games in a row. He was named the Most

Valuable Player three times. Other Italian sports stars include boxer Rocky Marciano, football player Joe Montana, football coach Vince Lombardi, and race-car driver Mario Andretti.

Some of the world's most well-known entertainers have also been Italian Americans. Frank Sinatra was a famous singer and actor for more than 60 years. Madonna Louise Veronica Ciccone—better known simply as "Madonna"—is another singer from an Italian family.

Italian-American singer Frank Sinatra

Madonna is just one of many Italian-American entertainers.

Al Pacino (sitting) and Marlon Brando in The Godfather

Italian Americans have appeared in movies, too. Robert de Niro and Al Pacino are two of the most famous. They both starred in the *Godfather* movies. These movies were about Mafia families. They were directed by Francis Ford Coppola, another talented Italian American. Frank Capra was also a famous director. He made some of America's favorite movies, including *It Happened One Night*, *It's a Wonderful Life*, and *Mr. Smith Goes to Washington*.

Italian Americans have been successful in business, too. Amadeo Peter Giannini started the Bank of America. Today, it is one of the largest banks in the world. He was one of the first people to loan money to Italian immigrants. After the San Francisco earthquake of 1906, many banks closed. Giannini put a desk on a pier and he was open for business!

Lee Iacocca made important contributions to the car industry. He helped design the famous Ford Mustang. He was the president of Chrysler Corporation, and he saved the company when it was having financial problems. Iacocca was in charge when the Statue of Liberty celebrated its 100th birthday in 1986.

Peter Gianinni, founder of the Bank of America

Lee Iacocca in a Chrysler convertible

Interesting Fact

▶ Between 1892 and 1954, more than 20 million people came into the United States at Ellis Island. More than 4 million of them were Italian.

Enrico Fermi, winner of the 1938 Nobel Prize for physics

Italians have also been scientists and inventors. Guglielmo Marconi developed the wireless **telegraph**—the invention that led to the radio. Enrico Fermi won the 1938 **Nobel Prize** in physics, a worldwide honor. He was also part of the team that made the first atomic bomb.

Many well-known politicians have been Italian. Fiorello La Guardia was the mayor of New York City three times. Geraldine Ferraro was the first woman nominated to run for vice president. Mario Cuomo was

Italian-American politicians Rudolph Giuliani (left) and Mario Cuomo (right)

Italian Americans have contributed a great deal to U.S. culture, as well as its kitchens.

the governor of New York State. Rudolph Giuliani twice served as mayor of New York City.

America has been a land of opportunity for many Italians. Today, Italians live throughout the country and they work in all kinds of jobs. They are part of the American family.

Prejudice, Sacco, and Vanzetti

ITALIAN IMMIGRANTS OFTEN HAD TO DEAL WITH PREJUDICE IN AMERICA. THIS MEANT that people did not trust them or like them simply because they were Italian. Sometimes Italians were kept out of good jobs. Other times, they were not paid as much as other workers doing the same job. They often lived in the worst neighborhoods. Many banks would not lend them money. Italians were often called insulting names. However, one of the worst examples of prejudice in U.S. history was the Sacco and Vanzetti trial.

In the 1920s, many Italians were active in labor unions. They wanted equal pay and better working conditions. Some Italian immigrants even became anarchists. They did not respect government authority.

During the 1920s, many Americans worried that there were too many immigrants. They especially did not like immigrants who tried to change things. Italian immigrants, particularly anarchists, were unpopular.

On April 15, 1920, two men were killed in a robbery in Massachusetts. Two Italian Americans were arrested. Their names were Nicola Sacco and Bartolomeo Vanzetti (left). There was no proof that these men had been involved in the killings, but they were Italian and they were anarchists. The lawyer who was prosecuting them could not prove they were guilty. He said Sacco and Vanzetti would have been able to kill, because they were Italian. The judge decided they were guilty and sentenced them to death.

People all over the world were upset by the trial. The Italian government asked to have the sentence changed. It was not. On August 23, 1927, Sacco and Vanzetti were executed.

1300s The Renaissance begins in Italy.

1600s Skilled Italian craftsworkers begin moving to America.

1800s Italians from northern Italy settle on the West Coast of the United States.

1805 Lorenzo da Ponte arrives in the United States. He later helps found the Italian Opera House in New York City.

1870 Italy becomes one country.

1880 Poor Italians from the Mezzagiorno come to America.

1889 Mother Cabrini arrives in New York City.

1892 Ellis Island opens in New York Harbor. Between 1892 and 1954, about 4 million Italian immigrants pass through Ellis Island.

1906 The San Francisco earthquake forces many of the city's banks to close.

1917 Mother Cabrini dies.

1922 Benito Mussolini becomes leader of Italy.

1927 Nicola Sacco and Bartolomeo Vanzetti are executed for a crime they probably did not commit.

1934 Fiorello La Guardia becomes major of New York City and serves until 1945.

1938 Enrico Fermi wins the Nobel Prize in physics.

1939 World War II begins in Europe.

1940 Italy enters World War II, siding with Germany.

1941 The United States enters World War II, siding with Great Britain.

1945 World War II ends.

1946 The Catholic Church declares Mother Cabrini a saint.

1982 Mario Cuomo is elected governor of New York State and serves until 1994.

1984 Geraldine Ferraro joins the Walter Mondale ticket and runs for vice president of the United States; they are defeated by Ronald Reagan and George H. W. Bush.

1986 Lee Iacocca oversees the 100th anniversary celebration of the Statue of Liberty.

1994 Rudolph Giuliani is elected major of New York City and serves through 2001.

ancestors (AN-sess-turs)
Ancestors are members of a family who lived a long time ago. Many of today's Americans had ancestors in Italy.

cholera (KOL-er-uh
Cholera is a dangerous disease that causes severe sickness and diarrhea. Cholera killed a large number of Italian people in the 1800s.

colony (KOL-uh-nee)
A colony is a territory that has been settled by people from another country and is controlled by that country. When the Italians first arrived in America, it was still a British colony.

discrimination (diss-krim-ih-NAY-shuhn)
Discrimination is an unjust behavior to others based on differences in age, race, gender, or other factors. For many years, Italian-Americans had to face discrimination in the United States.

drought (DROWT)
A drought is a long period of very dry weather. In the 1800s, many Italians lost their crops because of drought.

GI Bill (JEE EYE BIL)
The GI Bill was signed in 1944. It helped provide housing and education to people who had served in the military. A number of Italian Americans benefited from the GI Bill.

immigrants (IM-ih-grents)
Immigrants are people who come from a country to live permanently in another country. Italians were one group of immigrants who chose to make America their new home.

Nobel Prize (noh-BEL PRIZE)
Nobel Prizes are international awards given each year for excellence in literature, economics, medicine, physics, chemistry, and for promoting peace. Enrico Fermi won the Nobel Prize for physics in 1938.

philosophy (fih-LOSS-uh-fee)
Philosophy is the study truth, wisdom, and knowledge to gain an understanding of how life should be lived. The philosophy of Philip Mazzei inspired Thomas Jefferson when he wrote the Declaration of Independence.

prejudice (PREJ-uh-diss)
Prejudice is the hatred or unfair treatment that results from having fixed opinions about some group of people. In spite of the prejudice they were subjected to in the United States, Italian Americans worked hard in their new country.

telegraph (TEL-uh-graf)
A telegraph is a device or system for sending messages over long distances. It uses a code of electrical signals sent by wire or radio. Guglielmo Marconi developed the wireless telegraph.

For Further INFORMATION

Web Sites

Visit our homepage for lots of links about Italian Americans:
http://www.childsworld.com/links.html

Note to Parents, Teachers, and Librarians:
We routinely verify our Web links to make sure they're safe,
active sites—so encourage your readers to check them out!

Books

Bartone, Elisa. *Peppe the Lamplighter.* New York: Lothrop, Lee & Shepard, 1993.

Bunting, Eve. *A Picnic in October.* New York: Harcourt Brace, 1999.

Di Franco, J. Philip. *The Italian Americans.* New York: Chelsea House Publishers, 1995.

Fahey, Kathleen. *The Italians.* New York: Crabtree Publishing, 2000.

Hoobler, Dorothy and Thomas. *The Italian American Family Album.* New York: Oxford University Press Children's Books, 1998.

Petrini, Catherine M. *The Italian-Americans.* Minneapolis: Lerner, 2001.

Places to Visit or Contact

The American-Italian Heritage Association
P.O. Box 3136
Albany, NY 12203-0136
518-435-0591

Museo Italo Americano
Fort Mason Center, Building C
San Francisco, CA 94123
415-673-2200

The National Italian American Foundation
1860 19th Street, N.W.
Washington, DC 20009
202-387-0600

31

Index